OUR SIN
AND
THE SAVIOR

COMPACT EXPOSITORY PULPIT COMMENTARY SERIES

OUR SIN
AND
THE SAVIOR

Understanding the Need for Renewing
and Sanctifying Grace

DAVID A. HARRELL

© 2019 David A. Harrell

ISBN 978-1-7343452-0-9

Great Writing Publications, 425 Roberts Road, Taylors, SC 29687 www.greatwriting.org

Shepherd's Fire 5245 Highway 41-A Joelton, TN 37080 www.shepherdsfire.com

All Scripture quotations, unless stated otherwise, are taken from the New American Standard Bible® (NASB), Copyright © 1960, 1962, 1963, 1968, 1971, 1972, 1973, 1975, 1977, 1995 by The Lockman Foundation. Used by permission. www.Lockman. org All rights reserved.

No part of this publication may be reproduced, or stored in a retrieval system, or transmitted, in any form or by any means, mechanical, electronic, photocopying, recording or otherwise, without the prior permission of the publishers.

Shepherd's Fire exists to proclaim the unsearchable riches of Christ through mass communications for the teaching ministry of Bible expositor David Harrell, with a special emphasis in encouraging and strengthening pastors and church leaders.

Table of Contents

Books in this Series 6

Sin: Nature or Nurture? 7

The Spin on Sin 16

Holiness: The Antithesis of Sin 28

Sin and the Individual 46

Repentance and the Narrow Gate 56

Marks of Genuine Repentance 72

Eternal Wrath and Grace 80

Endnotes 87

Books in this Series

Finding Grace in Sorrow: Enduring Trials with the Joy of the Holy Spirit

Finding Strength in Weakness: Drawing Upon the Existing Grace Within

Glorifying God in Your Body: Seeing Ourselves from God's Perspective

God, Evil, and Suffering: Understanding God's Role in Tragedies and Atrocities

God's Gracious Gift of Assurance: Rediscovering the Benefits of Justification by Faith

Our Sin and the Savior: Understanding the Need for Renewing and Sanctifying Grace

The Marvel of Being in Christ: Adoring God's Loving Provision of New Life in the Spirit

The Miracle of Spiritual Sight: Affirming the Transforming Doctrine of Regeneration

1

Sin: Nature or Nurture?

The phone rang just after lunch. All I heard was, "Pastor . . ." Then uncontrollable sobs. When the woman gained composure, I recognized that she was one of mine—one of the precious sheep in my flock, along with her husband and four children. In between long periods of gut-wrenching anguish, she began to tell me what had happened. Her husband of many years had been arrested on drug-related charges and soliciting a prostitute who just happened to be an undercover policewoman. Obviously, she was devastated. As though she was trapped in a nightmare, she was unable to function. Fearing she may be suicidal, I immediately made arrangements with some key people to meet my wife and me at her home. I'll never forget the look on the face of the children. All any of us could do was cry. Like football players in a giant huddle, we all hugged, wept, and prayed. It was worse than a death.

Within hours, we discovered that what she told me was just the tip of the iceberg, which is almost always the case in such situations. Gambling debts, financial ruin, drug abuse, deceit, religious hypocrisy, years of pornography, immorality, physical abuse—the list went on. Now the husband faced prison time, while the humiliated and grief-stricken wife and children faced the unknown, asking questions such as, "Why?" "What happened?" and "How can this be?"

As a pastor, I have encountered tragedies like this more times than I care to remember. That's why I utterly loathe soap operas and reality shows. But every day, we witness human beings doing things that seemingly have no explanation. Shocking images of human brutality and lawlessness bombard our senses every time we turn on the news. From the disgraceful antics in the political arena to everyday road rage, no quarter is exempt from the degradation caused by human selfishness, greed, and deviancy. As if man is constantly doing battle with some kind of primal instinct that drives him to do evil, wickedness abounds. At every turn, people betray a deep dissatisfaction with themselves and the world in which they live, fueling an insatiable appetite for satisfaction at all costs. Man never has enough. Contentment is an illusion. Even those who are wealthy and have all the pleasures of the world available to them at the snap of their fingers can still lead miserable lives and commit horrible crimes.

But why? Why would the man in my example do what he did? Why would his wife conceal all that wickedness until it finally exploded? Why do the vast majority of people consistently act in their best interests despite the harm they cause to themselves and to others? Why are we all seemingly incapable of restraining ourselves from impulses that we know will bring misery? Why will we deliberately choose a certain course of action, knowing full well it is wrong? Why are we so prone to immorality, greed, slander, lying, violence, and war? Would anyone dare to argue that an individual's capacity for evil has no boundary? We need not look at the atrocities of Auschwitz to be convinced of this; we see this destructive force in our own life. And what is this force? *Sin.*

In 1887, one of the most compelling and powerful descriptions of sin that I have ever read was published:

It is a debt, a burden, a thief, a sickness, a leprosy, a plague, poison, a serpent, a sting; everything that man hates it is; a load of curses, and calamities beneath whose crushing most intolerable pressure, the whole creation groaneth . . .

Who is the hoary sexton that digs man a grave? Who is the painted temptress that steals his virtue? Who is the murderess that destroys his life? Who is this sorceress that first deceives, and then damns his soul?—Sin. Who, with icy breath, blights the fair blossoms of youth? Who breaks the hearts of parents? Who brings old men's grey hairs with sorrow to the grave?—Sin.

Who, by a more hideous metamorphosis than Ovid even fancied, changes gentle children into vipers, tender mothers into monsters and their fathers into worse than Herods, the murderers of their own innocents?—Sin.

Who casts the apple of discord on household hearts? Who lights the torch of war, and bears it blazing over trembling lands? Who, by divisions in the church, rends Christ's seamless robe?—Sin.

Who is this Delilah that sings the Nazirite asleep and delivers up the strength of God into the hands of the uncircumcised? Who, with winning smiles on her face, honey flattery on her tongue, stands in the door to offer the sacred rites of hospitality and, when suspicion sleeps, treacherously pierces our temples with a nail? What fair siren is this who, seated on a rock by the deadly pool, smiles to deceive, sings to lure, kisses to betray, and flings her arm around our neck to leap with us into perdition?—Sin.

Who turns the soft and gentlest heart to stone? Who hurls reason from her lofty throne, and impels sinners, mad as Gadarene swine, down the precipice, into a lake of fire?—Sin.[1]

So we must ask, is it merely ignorance and immaturity that causes people to be self-willed and cruel? Has their environment predisposed them to sin? If so, you would think with the level of sophistication humanity has achieved by now, we would be able to properly address these issues and train people to at least obey the elusive golden rule: "Do unto others as you would have them do unto you." But obviously this is not the case.

Why is it that as every infant matures, without any training or influence, he naturally develops a frightening attitude of selfishness that demands satisfaction of his every desire, no matter how foolish? Every honest parent will admit that, left unchecked, a child would destroy himself and anyone else who failed to meet his demands were he able to do so. No one needs to teach a child to be ill-tempered, impatient, demanding, selfish, jealous, violent, and utterly ruled by his lusts and emotions; he comes by it naturally. But why? Why is it that within every precious infant there exist the seeds of every imaginable form of evil—seeds of sins for which the damned are now tormented? Is it *nature*, or *nurture*? Are we *depraved*, or *deprived*?

Thankfully, our Creator answers this in great detail in His revelation to man in His inspired and infallible Word, the Bible. And as we examine the Scriptures, we learn very quickly that man does not act wickedly because of *nurture*, but because *his very nature is evil*. This is not to say that nurturing has no impact. It does. We see this principle in Proverbs 22:6 where we are admonished to "train up a child in the way he should go, even when he is old he will not depart from it." The apostle Paul also warned, "Do not be deceived: 'Bad company corrupts good morals'" (1 Cor. 15:33). But the consistent theme of Scripture is that although other forces will constantly exert themselves upon us, we will naturally be ruled by "the lusts of our flesh, indulging the desires of the flesh and of the mind, and [are] by nature children of wrath" (Eph. 2:3); we are "dead in our transgressions" (v. 5) and in desperate need of the mercy of God, who alone can make us "alive together with Christ" (v. 5).

God has revealed to us a stunning reality. One event radically altered the very nature of man and the planet on which he would live. That event was the deliberate rebellion of the first man He created, Adam. Because of Adam's sin in the garden, the entire human race was plunged into sin (Rom. 5:12) and every child is conceived in a state of sin and depravity. The Psalmist put it this way: "Behold, I was brought forth in iniquity, and in sin my mother conceived me" (Ps. 51:5). Sin has penetrated and corrupted the whole of man's being (Isa. 1:6; Eph. 4:17-19), including his body (Rom. 8:10), his mind (Rom. 8:6; 1 Cor. 2:14; 4:4; Titus 1:15), his will (John 8:34; Jer. 13:23; Rom. 7:18), and his heart (Jer. 17:9).

Every person is capable of committing the very worst sins (Rom. 1:18ff; 3:10-18); and apart from the transforming grace of God in salvation, even when the unsaved individual does right, it is for motivations other than to glorify God, making such actions displeasing to Him (Matt. 6:5: 2 Tim. 3:4). Worse yet, the unsaved are utterly bereft of that love for God necessary to fulfill the most basic requirement of God's moral law to love Him supremely (Deut. 6:4; 1 John 4:7-10). God has made it clear that the unregenerate will continue to spiral downward in morality (2 Tim. 3:13; Rom. 7:23) and they have no possible means of salvation or recovery within themselves (Matt. 19:25,26; Rom. 1:18; Eph. 2:1,8).

Sin is therefore *man's innate inability to conform to the moral character and desires of God.* John says, "sin is lawlessness" (1 John 3:4), which is not only a failure to obey God's moral law, but living as if it does not exist. It is a violation of the foremost commandment to "love the Lord your God with all your heart, and with all your soul, and with all your mind" (Matt. 22:37, *cf.* v. 38).

Sin is manifested primarily in human self-will—the root cause of all sin—fueled by the cherished lies of justified rebellion against God. People prefer to obey their wills rather than God's will. This is portrayed in Scripture as "the deeds of the flesh" and it includes things like, "immorality, impurity, sensuality, idolatry, sorcery, enmities, strife, jealousy, outbursts of anger, disputes, dissensions, factions, envying, drunkenness, carousing, and things like these . . . those who practice such things shall not inherit the kingdom of God" (Gal. 5:19-21). Because man is innately a slave to his sin (Rom. 6:16-20), he rejects his Creator, causing God to gradually abandon him to pursue the lusts of his heart and experience the devastating consequences of his iniquities, bringing him either to ruin or repentance (Rom. 1:24-32).

It is therefore the purpose of this book to examine these matters in the light of divine revelation and view them through the lens of humble faith, that we might better understand the marvelous mystery of the cross and deepen our love for the Lover of our souls.

2

The Spin on Sin

Many modern-day pastors bent on attracting "seekers" tend to define sin in such a way that virtually no one could be offended. The essence of their definition is that *sin includes all those things we think and do that rob us of fellowship with God and steal away the happiness He wants us to enjoy.* The good news of the gospel is then reduced to nothing more than God loving us so much that *He sent His Son to save us from our unhappiness.* Describing sin apart from the offended righteousness of God is not just irresponsible; it is heretical. Apart from an understanding of man's condemnation that evokes the wrath of God, the gospel is no gospel at all.

Most "seekers" are not told that sin is the defining characteristic of their very nature and that it is their innate inability to conform to God's moral character and desires. They are not told that all they *are* and *do* is fundamentally offensive to a holy God, rendering them guilty before His bar of justice and damned to an eternal hell; that "all have sinned and fall short of the glory of God" (Rom. 3:23), and that we must be "justified as a gift by His grace through the redemption which is in Christ Jesus; whom God displayed publicly as a propitiation in His blood through faith" (vv. 24-25). They are not warned that because of their innate corruption, they are not only alienated from God and subject to His wrath, but are also utterly unable to save themselves.

While teaching a three-week course in a seminary in Kenya, a group of people from a popular "seeker sensitive" mega-church in the United States came to spend the night on campus. The next day I had an opportunity to chat with some of them seated around me on a two-hour bus ride to visit a certain village. During the ride they asked me what I was teaching and I said, "I'm teaching a course on soteriology, the doctrine of salvation." They we're immediately fascinated and started asking many questions. But within a matter of minutes I discovered how little they understood about the Bible and basic theology.

For example, none of them believed in the doctrine of total and universal depravity of man—that we are counted guilty and have a sin nature because of Adam's sin. None of them believed that salvation was by *grace alone* through *faith alone* in *Christ alone.* They all insisted that man contributes to his salvation and that "there are many ways to heaven." And none of them believed in a *literal hell*. While some believed "really bad people" are annihilated when they die, others insisted that all people go to heaven, because, as one man put it, "God is love, and a loving God would never send anyone to hell." He then added: "I don't want anything to do with a God who would torture people!"

Obviously, they were clueless about the gospel! Without a soul-terrifying fear of God's just judgment, who needs "the Lamb of God who takes away the sin of the world" (John 1:29)? Like many today with an inflated opinion of their perceived righteousness, they would scoff at Solomon's analysis of man's depraved condition when he declared, "The hearts of the sons of men are full of evil, and insanity is in their hearts throughout their lives" (Eccl. 9:3).

Yet any honest evaluation of our own character and conduct gives irrefutable evidence of how our self-will is hopelessly prone to evil. But because of our depraved nature, we believe just the opposite. It is axiomatic for man to perceive himself as being innately *selfless*, not *selfish*, and *good*, not *evil*. If you challenge this self-righteous evaluation, you will start a fight every time. It is for this reason many evangelical churchmen have opted for a less incendiary theology—one that is more positive, more religiously and politically correct.

While the biblical doctrine of sin can be heard in some religious circles, it is altogether unheard of in the public forum. Imagine the outrage if a Christian politician were to suggest that college curricula for public educators include a biblical course explaining our children's sinful nature and the myriad of ways it can manifest itself? The reaction would be violent. Apoplectic with rage, objectors would scream, "Every child's relentless quest for self-esteem must be guarded against such Christian lunacy." They would argue that to suggest a child's human nature is so depraved that he lives under the sentence of divine wrath is the very worst kind of child abuse; such a cruel doctrine, they would say, does irreparable damage to his fragile self-image and produces unnecessary guilt and debilitation in the human psyche.

While such a reaction is expected among non-Christians with no capacity to discern spiritual realities (1 Cor. 2:14), it is appalling to think that many professing Christians also resent these inspired truths. *There is perhaps no greater example of beguiling deceit in the church today than the distortions surrounding the doctrine of sin and the power of the gospel to save.* Unfortunately, when sin is whitewashed, the Savior becomes irrelevant. Why take an antibiotic if you have no reason to believe you have an infection, especially if the doctor you trust says you're healthy? Given the increasingly shallow definitions of sin in our modern era of evangelical apostasy, especially as they relate to the presentation of the gospel message and issues relevant to Christian living, it is crucial that we carefully examine the Scriptures to understand exactly what sin really is, what it really looks like, and why it is so devastating and worthy of divine condemnation and death.

Sin in the Unregenerate heart

In the first three chapters of Romans (chapters 1 through 3:20), the apostle Paul exposed both the *potential* and *real* evil that resides in the sin nature of those outside of Christ in order to explain why they are under divine condemnation and in need of saving grace. The picture is frightening. He describes them as those who "suppress the truth in unrighteousness, because that which is known about God is evident within them; for God made it evident to them. For since the creation of the world His invisible attributes, His eternal power and divine nature, have been clearly seen, being understood through what has been made, so that they are without excuse" (Rom. 1:18b-20). Naturally His wrath is kindled due to their insolent rebellion against His character and the revelation of Himself through creation, conscience, and His Word (v. 18a).

Because of determined rejection, He therefore abandons them to the consequences of their fleshly lusts. Paul describes this present form of wrath (in contrast to eternal wrath) in his repeated use of the phrase "God gave them over" (Rom. 1:24, 26, 28)—a very strong verb in Greek *(paradidomi)* meaning to "deliver up" or "hand over," a judicial term often used in the New Testament to refer to one being delivered into the hands of another for punishment, even as Pilate did with Jesus: "but after having Jesus scourged, *he delivered Him* to be crucified" (Matt. 27:16, emphasis added; *cf.* Luke 21:12). Paul's use of this term in Romans 1 pertains to those who persistently reject God's revelation of Himself through creation and conscience and are therefore *given over* to the hideous torments of sin. Some have properly called this *the wrath of divine abandonment*. Here, God removes all restraint and protection in such people's lives, allowing their sinful choices to cause them to spiral down into utter ruin in an effort to bring them to repentance, as illustrated in Jesus' parable of the prodigal son in Luke 15.

As every Christian has witnessed, the inevitable corruption of sin will ultimately destroy those who reject the gospel of grace. The process can be heartbreaking, especially in the case of family members. We have all watched those we love make choices that directly oppose the will of God, resulting in every conceivable form of sorrow. I experience this on a weekly basis as a pastor as I counsel individuals whose lives have been totally decimated either because of their sin, or someone else's. Like ancient Israel's spiritual harlotry (Hos. 8:11), in helpless horror we watch people sow the wind only to reap the whirlwind. Yet in the drunken stupor of their sin, they experience no guilt and desire no remedy. To be sure, the man who does not understand the dreadful state of his condition cannot be saved, and, unless he repents, God will abandon him eternally.

In Romans 1, Paul describes a three-stage progression to divine abandonment, not necessarily found in every individual, but in the collective whole of the culture that magnifies individual wickedness. Each stage becomes progressively worse in its evil and in its consequence. The first stage is that of sordid immorality (vv. 24-25), the second stage results in shameless homosexuality (vv. 26-27), and the final outcome is shocking depravity in every area of life and society (vv. 28-32).

It is important to remember that the wellspring of such evil is in the *heart* of individuals. Scripture describes the *heart* as the seat of *emotions* (Prov. 23:17; 27:11; 69:20), and of the *intellect* (Ps. 4:4; Prov. 3:3; Luke 2:19), and of the *volitional* and *moral* life of man (Gen. 8:21; Prov. 6:18; Ps. 51:10). The heart is the very core of who we are, our inner person. It is from this innermost region of our personhood that our *conscience* warns, accuses or defends; our *mind* conceives, meditates, and discerns; our *will* makes choices and acts upon them; and our *emotions* respond in subjective approval or disapproval.

It is *not* our environment or circumstances that cause us to sin, as many misguided experts would have us believe. Nor is it some personality disorder. It is sin enthroned upon the heart of the unregenerate man who has "no fear of God before [his] eyes" (Rom. 3:18). And for the believer, it is the unredeemed sinful flesh waging war against the new nature, "for the flesh sets its desire against the Spirit, and the Spirit against the flesh; for these are in opposition to one another, so that you may not do the things that you please" (Gal. 5:17). James stated this clearly: "Each one is tempted when he is carried away and enticed by his own lust. Then when lust has conceived, it gives birth to sin; and when sin is accomplished, it brings forth death. Do not be deceived, my beloved brethren" (James 1:14-16).

Because he is enslaved by his sin, unregenerate man needs a new spiritual heart (Rom. 6:17-18). He needs to be *supernaturally transformed*, not *psychologically informed*. He needs to be sanctified by the truth of the Word (John 17:17), not by the presumed wisdom of some therapist. Man's problem is *spiritual*, not *psychological*. Jesus made this clear when He said, "Out of the heart come evil thoughts, murders, adulteries, fornications, thefts, false witness, slanders" (Matt. 15:19).

The Heinous Effects of Sin

Notwithstanding popular opinion, not only is sin man's innate inability to conform to the moral character and desires of God, but it is an evil so heinous that the first human sin committed by Adam plunged the entire human race into its vortex of destruction. For by "one man sin entered into the world, and death through sin, and so death spread to all men, because all sinned" (Rom. 5:12). Because of Adam's sin, his entire progeny is conceived in a state of depravity (Ps. 51:5), and therefore stand guilty and condemned before an infinitely holy God (John 3:18, 36). Then, to make matters worse, our adversary the devil "prowls about like a roaring lion, seeking someone to devour" (1 Peter 5:8), blinding unbelievers from the "the light of the gospel of the glory of Christ" (2 Cor. 4:4), murdering and deceiving (John 8:44), tempting (1 Thess. 3:5), and ensnaring us in every imaginable kind of sin (1 Tim. 3:7). In fact, "the whole world lies in the power of the evil one" (1 John 5:19). Because of this, man is in desperate need of salvation from the power, penalty, and presence of sin.

In light of all this, can there be a more important subject to consider than the innate sinfulness of man and its remedy in the transforming gospel of God? Is there a topic more worthy of our concern, given its implications for life on earth and beyond? Is there any doctrine more important to be precisely understood and preached by the church of Jesus Christ? I think not. In his *Theological Essays*, William G. T. Shedd poignantly summarized the vital importance of understanding man's intrinsic rebellion against God found in his nature when he said:

> . . . we cannot think, with some, that such speculations into a difficult doctrine like that of original sin, are valueless—that they merely baffle the mind and harden the heart. We rise from this investigation [into the doctrine of

original sin] with a more profound belief than ever, in the doctrine of the innate and total depravity of man—of his bondage to evil, and his guilt in this bondage. It is only when we turn away our eye from the particular exhibitions of sin to that evil nature that lies under them all, and lies under them all the while—it is only when we turn from what we do to what we are—that we become filled with that deep sense of guilt, that profound self-abasement, before the infinite purity of God, and that utter self-despair, which alone fit us to be the subjects of renewing and sanctifying grace. . . . If the current theology of the day is lacking in any one thing, it is in that thorough going. . . truly edifying theory of sin which runs like a strong muscular cord through all the soundest theology of the church.[2]

Since God has gone to such incredible lengths to both forgive and judge sin, it is obvious that sin is of monumental importance to Him, and it should be for us as well. It was for this reason that the Son of Man died a violent death of sacrifice and substitution, and later declared that the Holy Spirit would come, "to convict the world concerning sin, and righteousness, and judgment" (John 16:8). Furthermore, when we consider the cosmic effects of God's curse upon His creation because of Adam's sin (Gen. 3:14-24; *cf.* Rom. 8:19-23), His wrath poured out upon His Son, and the horrors of hell, we get some sense of how inconceivably vile it is to His holy nature. For this reason, it is important to first understand the holiness of God—the antithesis of sin—in order to fully understand the nature of sin.

3

Holiness: The Antithesis of Sin

It stands to reason that if the sinfulness of man is trivialized, the same fate will befall an understanding of the holiness of God. Both ends of the spectrum must be equally infinite—holiness in its transcendent purity, and sin in its vile corruption. To mitigate one is to diminish the other. Both must be held in equal tension at both ends of the spectrum of good and evil. The apostle Paul understood this. He acknowledged his deep love and respect for the holiness of God manifested in His Law when he declared, "I joyfully concur with the law of God in the inner man" (Rom. 7:22). Therefore, because of his knowledge of the Holy One, the corrupting presence and power of indwelling sin was made even more apparent to him, causing him to say, "But I see a different law in the members of my body, waging war against the law of my mind and making me a prisoner of the law of sin which is in my members," to which he lamented, "Wretched man that I am! Who will set me free from the body of this death?" (vv. 23, 24).

Every believer must grasp this simple truth: *we will only see our sin in proportion to our willingness to see the holiness of God.* Said differently, if we have a low view of God, we will have a high view of self. When God is small, sin is insignificant. But when we see God as He really is—the thrice-holy Lord of hosts whose glory fills the earth (Isa. 6:3)—we will respond like Isaiah and cry out, "Woe is me, for I am ruined! Because I am a man of unclean lips, and I live among a people of unclean lips; for my eyes have seen the King, the Lord of hosts" (v. 5).

This is the kind of vision every man needs—a vision of soul-terrifying purity that contrasts the staggering ugliness of sin. Only this will produce genuine repentance and willing sacrifice (v. 8). We must see ourselves as God sees us. Such a perspective will instantly end any thought of inherent goodness, because nothing human can possibly endure the white-hot light of divine holiness without being instantly incinerated. Only in Scripture and in the person of His Son can a man behold the transcendent, indescribable perfections of the Most High God. And in the glow of that vision, every man will gasp at the sheer horror of his sin, resulting in a self-loathing and a thirst for God. Worshipful obedience then becomes a passionate desire, not a burdensome duty—a craving of the soul animated by a breathless adoration of the One who deserves our utmost.

Naturally, those who are ignorant of God's revelation of Himself and indifferent about matters He deems sacred will show little, if any, remorse over violating His standards for righteousness. The unsaved are well served by a shallow definition of both holiness and sin, allowing them to live comfortably according to their own standards. This is also true among nominal "Christians" whose irreverent lives mirror unbelievers who love the world—that Satanic system determined to thwart the purposes of God at every turn (*cf.* 1 John 5:19). Naturally, the effect of disrespected holiness manifests itself in the worldly lives they lead, calling into question the authenticity of their faith which is determined by what a man *does*, not what he *professes*. A.W. Tozer made this insightful observation:

> The Church has surrendered her once lofty concept of God and has substituted for it one

so low, so ignoble, as to be utterly unworthy of thinking, worshiping men. This she has done not deliberately, but little by little and without her knowledge; and her very unawareness only makes her situation all the more tragic. The low view of God entertained almost universally among Christians is the cause of a hundred lesser evils everywhere among us. . . . With our loss of the sense of majesty has come the further loss of religious awe and consciousness of the divine Presence. We have lost our spirit of worship and our ability to withdraw inwardly to meet God in adoring silence.[3]

God has revealed that because man's nature is corrupt, fallen people are unholy and therefore incapable having a relationship with Him who is holy (Heb. 12:14). Because his "heart is deceitful above all things, and desperately wicked" (Jer. 17:9), a man must be supernaturally recreated. He needs a new heart, a completely new nature. As Jesus said, he must be "born again" (John 3:3); he must experience a spiritual rebirth to which he is wholly incapable of offering even the slightest contribution.

Only then can he have fellowship with God. And upon rightly seeing the majesty of the divine presence, he will falter under his burden of sin, and its weight will drive him to a sanctifying despair that will result in *regeneration — a supernatural and instantaneous impartation of spiritual life to the spiritually dead*. Never again will he offer an argument against his depraved nature. Then, having received the gift of faith, he will be lifted up by mercy and saved by grace. The Holy Spirit will set him apart unto God and infuse him with Christ's own likeness that will increasingly manifest itself in his character and conduct.

To Be Set Apart

The basic meaning of *holiness* (Hebrew: *qedosh*; Greek: *hagios*) is "set apart" or "separation." Morally speaking, anything that is "holy" is set apart or separated from sin and consecrated to God. For this reason, the Old Testament speaks frequently about maintaining the distinction between things that are sacred and those considered secular or worldly. Perhaps the greatest example of this can be found in the Tabernacle where every aspect of that ancient place of worship symbolized the priority of being separate from the world. Even within the Tabernacle, God ordained that the most holy place that housed the Ark of the Covenant be devoted solely to His service and separated from the sinfulness of the world by a "veil of blue and purple and scarlet material and fine twisted linen . . . made with cherubim, the work of a skillful workman" (Ex. 26:31).

Inside the Ark was the Holy Standard, the Law of Moses given on Sinai. Above the Ark on each end were golden cherubs with outstretched wings that symbolically guarded the holiness of God, and between the cherubs hovered the *shekinah* glory of God—the ineffable light of His presence, too brilliant to be seen by the fallen eyes of man. On top of the Ark was a golden lid that separated the law within from the Holy presence above, thus symbolizing that the Law had been violated and God's holiness cannot be contaminated by sin.

All of this had profound implications for sinful man who desired to be reconciled to a holy God, for it was upon this lid that divine justice and grace came together symbolically once every year on the Day of Atonement. This was the holiest of days when the High Priest sprinkled the blood of an animal on that golden lid of separation. That lid was called the "Mercy Seat," the *hilasterion* in the LXX (the Septuagint or Greek translation of the Old Testament)—the Greek term that means to *appease, placate,* or *satisfy*. This was the sacrifice of atonement. The same term was used in 1 John 2:1 to describe

"Jesus Christ the righteous; and He Himself is the propitiation (*hilasmos*) for our sins." Likewise we read in 1 John 4,

> . . . God has sent His only begotten Son into the world so that we might live through Him. In this is love, not that we loved God, but that He loved us and sent His Son to be the propitiation (*hilasmos*) for our sins (vv. 9b,10).

The amazing truth of the gospel of Christ was thereby foreshadowed in the sacrificial system. The Lord clarified this when He stated in Exodus 25:21,22:

> You shall put the mercy seat (*hilasterion*—LXX) on top of the ark, and in the ark you shall put the testimony which I will give to you. There I will meet with you; and from above the mercy seat, from between the two cherubim which are upon the ark of the testimony.

This Mercy Seat was the place where the just wrath of God was symbolically propitiated; where divine fury was temporarily appeased; where God's righteous anger was symbolically satisfied and His vengeance upon sinners temporarily placated.

Only the most hardened sinner or superficial Christian could possibly contemplate such a scene and remain insensitive to the transcendent holiness of God, His hatred of sin, and His uninfluenced mercy and grace offered to sinners through Jesus Christ, our Propitiation. For He was the One who "entered the Most Holy Place once for all, having obtained eternal redemption" (Heb. 9:12).

Indeed, the sheer holiness of these divine symbols and redemptive truths should stir every believer to a deep and solemn reverence for God and a personal pursuit of holiness. It should motivate our every thought and deed and also be readily apparent in corporate worship. Sadly, often this is not the case. Most worship services reflect indifferent hearts that have no desire for God and no appetite to enter into the transcendent, awe-inspiring presence of His glory. As if a deliberate rebellion against reverence had been ordered, everything from the way people dress, the musical genre, and even the sermon seem determined to trivialize holiness and cheapen grace by exalting frivolity and superficiality. Churches with this bent typically excuse and exalt Christians whose lives mirror the standards and values of the world.

The enormous weight God places upon separation can also be seen in the Old Testament Sabbath, the sign of the Mosaic Covenant (Ex. 31:16) and the dominating feature of the Law. We read in Exodus 20:11 that God "blessed the Sabbath day and made it holy." The Sabbath day included numerous restrictions (Ex. 16:29, 23; 20:10; 35:1-3; Jer. 17:27; Neh. 10:31; Isa. 58:13-14) that forced the Jews to reflect upon their inability to keep the Law and admit that their only hope of salvation was in God's undeserved mercy and uninfluenced grace. There were eleven other Sabbaths God required, each designed to remind the people of His holiness, their sin, and their need for a Savior.[4]

Along with the concept of separation, any definition of holiness must include the idea of *transcendence*, for indeed He is "the high and exalted One who lives forever, whose name is Holy, [who] dwell[s] on a high and holy place" (Isa. 57:15a). Holiness cannot be compared to anything we know, because all we know is unholy. Holiness is completely *other*, incomprehensible, and so unapproachable that even the seraphim who do His bidding cover their faces in His presence (Isa. 6:2). For the most part, holiness is undiscoverable apart from the illuminating work of the Spirit of God upon the heart of faith. It is therefore unspeakably transcendent. It is a mystery so vast, that apart from divine self-disclosure, it would remain forever unknown to us.

And even with the help of the inspired Scriptures, we still find ourselves lost in wonder. Yet God commanded His covenant people, Israel, "Be holy; for I am holy" (Lev. 11:44); and also, speaking to His church He said, "As obedient children, do not be conformed to the former lusts which were yours in your ignorance, but like the Holy One who called you, be holy yourselves also in all your behavior; because it is written, 'You shall be holy, for I am holy'" (1 Peter 1:14-16).

This indicates that *holiness primarily pertains to moral purity, being utterly separate from sin*. But a question naturally arises: "How can a man be holy when holiness is so obviously unattainable?" The answer is found in the imputation of the righteousness of Christ, making the gospel itself unequalled in its power to transform sinners into saints. Because of sin, man stands before the bar of divine justice and hears the verdict—*guilty!* Yet in the miracle of justification by faith, the sinless Savior stands in his place and assumes his guilt and bears his punishment. As a result, the believer is not merely *treated or even considered as righteous although he is still guilty*. No, this holy transaction is exceedingly more glorious. Instead, *the sinner is declared to be actually righteous* (Rom. 3:21-24)—a gift far beyond pardon, even beyond forgiveness. Such a radical transformation shouts of God's hatred of sin and man's need for a righteousness that is not his own.

Even as a man blind from birth has no conception of a sunrise, sinful man cannot see his need for righteousness because he has no concept of holiness. Sin being what it is rails against separation, transcendence, and moral purity. It is the ultimate force of blindness. In fact, sin produces the exact opposite. It foolishly elevates self-righteousness to the status of divine acceptance, thus illustrating his innate inability to conform to the moral character and desires of God.

Holiness and the Law

We also see God's holiness in His *Law*, which provides yet another stark contrast to the nature of sin. The Law of God, sometimes referred to as the Mosaic Code, was the codification of God's holiness, the divine standard of righteousness. Any breech or violation, no matter how small, was tantamount to breaking the whole law (Deut. 27:26; Gal. 3:10). The Law (which can also be understood as the Old Testament Scriptures) had three divisions. First, there was the *moral* law that regulated how Israel was to love the Lord with all their being and their neighbor as themselves, all of which was based upon the Ten

Commandments. Second was the *judicial* law that regulated the nation of Israel as a theocracy. And third was the *ceremonial* law that regulated Israel's worship. In his monumental work, "The Greatness of the Kingdom," Alva J. McClain made this perceptive assessment concerning the Law of God:

> Perhaps the outstanding characteristic of the Mosaic Code is found in its *indivisible unity* . . . . However, within the framework of this unity, there may be found at least three definite elements: religious, moral, and civil. This is as we might expect in a code which is to govern men in a kingdom of God upon the earth. For the total needs of men fall within three general categories: first, since man is a religious being, he needs to be guided in his relation to God; second, since man is a moral being, he needs to be informed as to the basic principles of right and wrong; and third, since he is a social and political being, he needs guidance in the details affecting such relationships. All the various aspects of the Mosaic Code fall within these three general realms; yet never separated into fragmentary and autonomous compartments of human existence, but always finding their indivisible

unity in God Himself as man's Creator and Sovereign.[5]

Ultimately, the Lord Jesus Christ fulfilled each division of the Law (Matt. 5:17). His sinless life fulfilled the *moral* law. His condemnation and temporary judgment upon Israel whereby they were temporarily set aside as a nation fulfilled the *judicial* Law. And finally, His atoning work on the cross fulfilled the *ceremonial* law. But we should not forget that while the *judicial* and *ceremonial* laws were fulfilled in Christ and are now obsolete, the *moral* law is still being fulfilled through the church because we are united to Christ through faith. The apostle Paul spoke of this sobering truth in Romans 8 where he reminds us that God sent "His own Son in the likeness of sinful flesh and as an offering for sin, He condemned sin in the flesh, in order that the requirement of the Law might be fulfilled in us, who do not walk according to the flesh, but according to the Spirit" (vv. 3-4).

In light of the incomprehensible holiness of God and the revelation of that holiness delineated in His Law and fulfilled in Christ, it is difficult to understand why so many people who name the name of Christ have so little respect for the sacred admonitions of His Word. Whether through sins of omission or commission, violating His divine standard of righteousness in our modern evangelical culture of tolerance and worldliness is simply no big deal. "After all," many will say, "grace covers it all."

But we must understand that sin is to God what radiation is to man—it is morally toxic, utterly abhorrent. We get a sense of this in Psalm 11:4-7 where David said,

> The Lord is in His holy temple; the Lord's throne is in heaven; His eyes behold, His eyelids test the sons of men. The Lord tests the righteous and the wicked, and the one who loves violence His soul hates. Upon the wicked He will rain snares; fire and brimstone and burning wind will be the portion of their cup. For the Lord is righteous; He loves righteousness; the upright will behold His face.

The antiphonal worship of the seraphim in Isaiah 6 further emphasizes the holiness of God when "one called out to another and said, 'Holy, Holy, Holy, is the Lord of hosts, the whole earth is full of His glory'" (v. 3). And in that vision, the prophet Isaiah was able to contrast the darkness of his sin against the penetrating light of divine holiness, causing him to cry out in sheer terror, "Woe is me, for I am ruined! Because I am a man of unclean lips, and I live among a people of unclean lips; for my eyes have seen the King, the Lord of hosts" (Isa. 6:5).

We must recognize that *holiness is the all-encompassing attribute of God*. It portrays His consummate perfection, His majesty, and His eternal glory. Like no other attribute He used to describe Himself in Scripture, holiness stands alone as the defining characteristic of His person. It alone is the quintessential summation of all His attributes. He is the great "I AM" (Ex. 3:14), the One who has life intrinsic *to* Himself and *in* Himself. He is utterly self-existent, eternal, and unchanging. He is absolutely separate from our nature, having a nature we cannot comprehend—one that is untainted by sin; in fact, He cannot sin, and neither can He tolerate sin. He is morally perfect in every conceivable way. Every thought, every action, every decree, every verdict, every judgment upon sin is always perfect and just. Every decision is absolutely righteous, as Abraham acknowledged when he said, "Shall not the Judge of all the earth deal justly?" (Gen. 18:25).

The Chasm Between Holiness and Sin

In light of all this, it should be obvious that *there is an infinite chasm between God's holiness and man's sin.* By nature, man resents God's sovereign authority over His creation and rebels against His law. Man does not naturally conform to the character and desires of God, because he is not holy. Man is not morally set apart from sin; he is the personification of it. God affirms this reality through His apostle when he says,

> There is none righteous, not even one; there is none who understands, there is none who seeks for God; all have turned aside, together they have become useless; there is none who does good, there is not even one. Their throat is an open grave, with their tongues they keep deceiving, the poison of asps is under their lips; whose mouth is full of cursing and bitterness; their feet are swift to shed blood, destruction and misery are in their paths, and the path of peace they have not known. There is no fear of God before their eyes (Rom. 3:10-18).

And what is worse, man can no more change his sinful nature than an ant can become an elephant or a leopard change his spots. Moreover, because God is holy, all sin must be punished. In fact, if God were not angry at sin, He would not be holy. For this reason, God's wrath is kindled against sinners, and in His judgment He is "a consuming fire" (Heb. 12:29). He will punish all who reject the gift of grace offered through His Son the Lord Jesus Christ—He "will burn up the chaff with unquenchable fire" (Luke 3:17c). The apostle Paul reminds us that "the wrath of God is revealed from heaven against all ungodliness and unrighteousness of men who suppress the truth in unrighteousness" (Rom. 1:18). Since "all have sinned and fall short of the glory of God" (Rom. 3:23), and because sinners cannot survive His judgment without a remedy for their sin, the gospel of Jesus Christ is good news beyond measure.

However, it is important to emphasize, again, that no one can ever appreciate the glorious gospel of Christ apart from understanding two essential truths: individuals must have a *profound mourning over the depths of their depravity and a soul-shocking grasp of the holiness of God*. Said simply, they must fear God, for "the fear of the Lord is the beginning of knowledge; fools despise wisdom and instruction" (Prov. 1:7). No sinner can be saved until he understands that he has violated the Law of God and offended His holiness. Sinful man must understand that he needs to be reconciled to God—to be made holy by the imputed righteousness of Christ, to be set apart from sin unto God. Therefore, *any gospel presentation that excludes these fundamental truths eviscerates the very heart of the gospel, thereby robbing God of His glory by disregarding His holiness and trivializing the sufferings of Christ.*

4

Sin and the Individual

We learn even more about the nature of sin by examining *how sin manifests itself in the individual*. Scripture reveals at least four distinct, yet overlapping, ways in which it can be seen in those who have not been transformed by the regenerating power of the Holy Spirit through repentant faith in the Lord Jesus Christ.

First, as stated earlier, we see sin as being *a state or disposition of the soul*. It is an intrinsic part of the very essence of man. David acknowledged his depraved disposition, saying, "Behold, I was brought forth in iniquity, and in sin my mother conceived me." His son Solomon concurred, saying, "the hearts of the sons of men are full of evil, and insanity is in their hearts throughout their lives" (Eccl. 9:3). Jeremiah made the point that "The heart is more deceitful than all else and is desperately sick; who can understand it?" (17:9). The apostle Paul gave further evidence of the effects of our fallen nature even after salvation when he said of himself, "For I know that nothing good dwells in me, that is in my flesh; for the willing is present in me, but the doing of the good is not. For the good that I want, I do not do, but I practice the very evil that I do not want. But if I am doing the very thing I do not want, I am no longer the one doing it, but sin which dwells in me" (Rom. 7:18-20).

In his classic work, *The Nature, Power, Deceit, and Prevalency of Indwelling Sin*, Puritan theologian John Owen addressed this unrelenting and powerful principle of indwelling sin in the believer when he said:

> It always abides in the soul—it is never absent. The apostle twice uses that expression, "It dwells in me." There is its constant residence and habitation. If it came upon the soul only at certain seasons much obedience might be perfectly accomplished in its absence; yea, and as they deal with usurping tyrants, whom they intend to thrust out of a city, the gates might be sometimes shut against it, that it might not return—the soul might fortify itself against it. But the soul is its home; there it dwells, and

is no wanderer. Wherever you are, whatever you are about, this law of sin is always in you; in the best that you do, and in the worst. Men little consider what a dangerous companion is always at home with them. When they are in company, when alone, by night or by day, all is one, sin is with them. There is a living coal continually in their houses; which, if it be not looked unto, will fire them, and it may be consume them. Oh, the woeful security of poor souls! How little do the most of men think of this inbred enemy that is never from home! How little, for the most part, does the watchfulness of any professors answer the danger of their state and condition![6]

SECONDLY, because sin is a state or disposition of the soul corrupting every aspect of man's nature, it manifests itself in his *thinking*. We see this in God's prohibition against things like covetousness (Ex. 20:17), hatred (Lev. 19:17), and lusting in our heart (Matt. 5:27-28)—all being sins of thought. Scripture makes it clear that unbelievers are spiritually "dead in [their] trespasses and sins" (Eph. 2:1) and have no capacity to comprehend spiritual truth (1 Cor. 2:14), for "both their mind and their conscience are defiled" (Titus 1:15c). Said simply, *man is a spiritual cadaver*. Unless a he experiences the miracle of the new birth in Christ, he will remain "darkened in [his] understanding, alienated from the life of God because of the ignorance that is in [him], due to [his] hardness of heart" (Eph. 4:18).

THIRDLY, the metastasizing corruption of sin manifests itself in man's *will*, making him a "slave to sin" (John 8:34). Because his will is in bondage to sin, man is obviously unable to change his sinful nature, depicted in the vivid analogy God used when He spoke through the prophet Jeremiah, saying, "Can the Ethiopian change his skin or the leopard his spots? Then you also can do good who are accustomed to doing evil" (Jer. 13:23; *cf.* Rom. 7:18). For this reason Jesus said, "This is the judgment, that the Light has come into the world, and men loved the darkness rather than the Light, for their deeds were evil" (John 3:19).

FOURTHLY, sin can manifest itself through *omission*. This is the unwitting failure to do what we ought to do. Sin has so permeated and corrupted the whole of our being that we frequently sin without having any awareness we have done so. For this reason the psalmist prayed, "Acquit me of hidden faults" (19:12), and James said, "Therefore, to one who knows the right thing to do and does not do it, to him it is sin" (4:17). The list of things that we ignorantly and unconsciously do that are displeasing to God are beyond our ability to fathom. Recognizing this, and knowing that it is ultimately God alone who can rightly discern and judge men's thoughts, Paul said, "I do not even examine myself. For I am conscious of nothing against myself, yet I am not by this acquitted; but the one who examines me is the Lord" (1 Cor. 4:3-4).

Similarly, David acknowledged, "For evils beyond number have surrounded me; my iniquities have overtaken me, so that I am not able to see; they are more numerous than the hairs of my head, and my heart has failed me" (Ps. 40:12).

When taking into consideration all the various biblical terms for sin and the different concepts used to depict how sin manifests itself, we arrive at the definition stated at the beginning of this chapter: *Sin is man's innate inability to conform to the moral character and desires of God.*

Total Depravity and Inability

As we have seen, the scope of sin's defilement of the individual is *complete*, often labeled "total depravity." There is no aspect of man's essence that has escaped sin's corruption. No human being ever born, except the God-man Jesus of Nazareth, has perfectly conformed to the moral character and desires of God.

This does not mean, however, that unsaved people will indulge in every form of wickedness and have no propensity to do things that are morally good. In fact, even the unregenerate have an innate sense of right and wrong and are able to practice virtuous acts such as compassion, justice, and honesty, and despise those who do otherwise. God has placed within every individual an intrinsic understanding of the basic tenets of His Law. This serves as a standard that activates the conscience, producing guilt that can lead to repentance, faith, and obedience. The apostle Paul described this fascinating reality when he said, "For when the Gentiles who do not have the Law do instinctively the things of the Law, these, not having the Law, are a law to themselves, in that they show the work of the Law written in their hearts, their conscience bearing witness and their thoughts alternately accusing or else defending them" (Rom. 2:14-15).

While it is true that even in his sinful nature unsaved man can do things that are morally good in the eyes of society, nevertheless, because he is utterly bereft of any genuine love for God, the most basic requirement of God's moral law (Deut. 6:4; 1 John 4:7-10), and because his motivations will never be to glorify God (Rom. 3:10-18; 2 Tim. 3:4), *even his most righteous deeds will not be pleasing to God.*

This tragic reality is sometimes referred to as man's "total inability." Many theologians prefer using the term *total inability* rather than *total depravity* which, unfortunately, can often be misunderstood to mean that unsaved people have no disposition whatsoever to do good. On the other hand, the concept of *total inability* accurately communicates the doctrinal issue at stake, namely, although the extent of sin's corruption is total, unregenerate individuals can nevertheless choose to act morally. However, because of a person's inability to love God supremely, combined with his inherent self-will, his actions cannot please God.

Isaiah described this when he lamented, "For all of us have become like one who is unclean, and all our righteous deeds are like a filthy garment" (64:6a); a description that is equally true for unbelievers (*cf.* Phil. 3:5-8). Paul also addressed this issue in Romans 8:8 when he said, "Those who are in the flesh cannot please God." As offensive as this doctrine may be to many people, God makes it abundantly clear that *there is nothing unregenerate man can do that merits God's approval.* This is because nothing he does proceeds from a heart of faith, and "without faith it is impossible to please Him" (Heb. 11:6).

As stated earlier, while most people define the nature of sin in terms of what we *do* rather than what we *are*, the overwhelming biblical evidence demonstrates that the scope of sin's defilement on the individual is so complete, that *apart from the transformation of the new birth in salvation, everything about man is displeasing to God and therefore he cannot give Him glory.*

And what is even more disturbing is that because of sin's power to deceive, man is utterly unaware of his condition, let alone the judgment that awaits him unless he repents and trusts in Christ as Savior. Satan's temptation of Eve was so cunning that she had no suspicion that her choices were evil. The ingenious deceptions of Satan are snares of temptations concealed in the well-worn paths of habitual sinfulness. The enemy of our soul works in concert with our depraved condition, as indicated in the apostle Paul's words in 2 Corinthians 4:3-4 where he said, "And even if our gospel is veiled, it is veiled to those who are perishing, in whose case the god of this world has blinded the minds of the unbelieving so that they might not see the light of the gospel of the glory of Christ, who is the image of God."

It is fascinating to consider that with all the amazing accomplishments of mankind with respect to science and technology, the ravages of evil upon the earth have not been mitigated in the slightest. *Man is not only as wicked as ever; he is more wicked than ever*. And God has promised that, with time, his vile estate will get worse, not better (2 Tim. 3:1, 13; Rom. 7:23). The moral freefall in America alone gives testimony to this trend.

The moral fibers of every society on earth are rotting because of sin's corrupting effects. Yet man continues to shake his puny little fist in God's face and dare Him to judge him. For this reason, "the wrath of God is revealed from heaven against all ungodliness and unrighteousness of men who suppress the truth in unrighteousness" (Rom. 1:18). And there is perhaps no greater evidence of God's wrath today than the wrath of His divine abandonment as He lifts His restraining grace from the wickedness of man and gives him over to the consequences of his iniquity. The tragic results of this are summarized in the words of the apostle Paul in Romans 1 when he stated,

> And just as they did not see fit to acknowledge God any longer, God gave them over to a depraved mind, to do those things which are not proper, being filled with all unrighteousness, wickedness, greed, evil; full of envy, murder, strife, deceit, malice; they are gossips, slander-

ers, haters of God, insolent, arrogant, boastful, inventors of evil, disobedient to parents, without understanding, untrustworthy, unloving, unmerciful; and although they know the ordinance of God, that those who practice such things are worthy of death, they not only do the same, but also give hearty approval to those who practice them (vv. 28-32).

It bears repeating yet again: before a man can possibly believe the gospel and trust Christ as Savior, it is essential that he have at least a basic understanding of his sin and God's holiness. At some fundamental level, even a child must understand that his sin is *the failure to conform to the moral character and desires of God*, and he is, therefore, totally unable to please God, totally unable to save himself, and totally unable to find any recovery within himself.

Man's sin nature camps on one side of an infinite chasm, and the holiness of God on the other. Herein is the unfathomable problem that the Triune God overcame in salvation. In His infinite wisdom, and because of His marvelous mercy, love, and grace, He made a way for wicked people to be reconciled to Himself through the transforming gospel of God that provides a way for Him to justify the ungodly.

5

Repentance and the Narrow Gate

Repentance is a foreign concept in our postmodern culture, even among professing evangelicals. It assumes the existence of a moral standard that has been violated and a righteous God that has been offended, neither of which is considered to be a valid presupposition in an age where *absolute* or *moral truth* has been rejected and replaced with a prevailing attitude of *skepticism, subjectivism,* and *relativism.*

In order to comprehend the doctrine of repentance, it is therefore crucial to understand the simple, yet profound, message of Jesus in Matthew 7:24-27. Here the Lord describes two men who each built a religious house: one wise, one foolish. Each house represents the two options of salvation

He described earlier in the chapter in verses 13-23. There He made it clear that every man who is invited to faith in Jesus Christ will face two options, both promising heaven. One will be true, the other false. The true way will be hard to enter; the false way will be easy. Few will even be able to find the narrow way, much less choose to enter through it. Instead, most will choose the false and easy way. Essentially, He warns that every person must choose between:

Two gates: narrow and wide;
Two ways: narrow and broad;
Two destinations: life and destruction;
Two groups: the few and the many — and these are likened to:

- Two kinds of trees: good and bad
- Two kinds of people who profess Christ: sincere and insincere
- Two kinds of spiritual builders: wise and foolish
- Two kinds of religious foundations: rock and sand
- Two kinds of houses of faith: one will stand the storms of final judgment; the other will collapse in a heap of eternal doom.

So what is the key to entering the narrow gate that leads to life that few will find and enter? The answer in a word: *repentance*. But this is far more than the voice of conscience bringing our sins to remembrance and causing us to feel ashamed. It is more than trembling with fear when contemplating the penalty of sin in eternal hell. It is more than a man attaching himself to some religious system and depending upon servile submission to that system to earn his way to heaven. It is more than tearfully confessing long lists of sins and temporarily renouncing them only to return to them again like a dog returns to its vomit. Instead, *true repentance is a God-induced hatred of sin, a turning from sin, and a Spirit-empowered forsaking of sin, resulting in a turning to God for mercy and grace.*

While repentance should never be considered a condition of salvation—for there are no conditions to grace—it is a crucial element of the gift of grace (Eph. 2:8). Belief in Christ and repentance are always inseparably linked and will inevitably result in a life that changes direction as in the case of the Gentiles "who believed" and "turned to the Lord" (Acts 11:21); it is produced within us by the Author of life who gives "the repentance that leads to life" (Acts 11:18). By His regenerating power, He gives us the gift of faith, the grace to believe, and we "in humility receive the word implanted, which is able to save [our] souls" (James 1:21).

Genuine repentance produces an appropriate and accurate sense of guilt that causes a man to beg for mercy and forgiveness of sin resulting in a change of mind and purpose whereby he turns from sin and turns toward God. This can be seen in the attitude of the tax collector recorded in Luke 18 who was so overwhelmed by the reality of his sin and unworthiness to be forgiven that he "was even unwilling to lift up his eyes to heaven, but was beating his breast, saying, 'God, be merciful to me, the sinner!'" (v. 13). D. Martyn Lloyd-Jones gave great clarity to the scope of repentance when a sinner comes to Christ when he said:

> Repentance means that you realize that you are a guilty, vile sinner in the presence of God, that you deserve the wrath and punishment of God, that you are hell-bound. It means that you begin to realize that this thing called sin is in you, that you long to get rid of it, and that you turn your back on it in every shape and form. You renounce the world whatever the cost, the world in its mind and outlook as well as its practice, and you deny yourself, and take up the cross and go after Christ. Your

nearest and dearest, and the whole world, may call you a fool, or say you have religious mania. You may have to suffer financially, but it makes no difference. That is repentance.[7]

To be sure, true repentance is far more than reformation where a person resolves to do better and turn over a new leaf in his life (*cf.* Matt. 12:43-45). It is far more than contrition where someone feels sorry for his sin and the misery it has caused in his life (*cf.* Luke 18:23). True repentance so grips such a person's heart with the fear of God as to cause him to hate his sin more than hell itself. And in his loathing over it, he desperately embraces the truth of the gospel of Christ as his only hope of salvation, and decisively commits to turning from sin, denying himself, and following Christ—even if it costs him his life. The essence of repentance that so few embrace cries out in desperation saying:

> Oh God, I see the horrors of my sin. There is nothing about me that conforms to Your moral character and desires. My life has been a constant violation of Your law. I have lived only unto myself. I have not feared You nor loved You with all my heart, soul,

mind, and strength. Indeed, I have not truly known the God of the Bible; instead, I have worshipped myself and gods of my own making. I have denied the Lord Jesus Christ with my hypocrisy. I have blasphemed His name by my adherence to false doctrine and religious deception. My heart has been calloused. My will has been obstinate. My life has been wasted. I stand guilty as charged. I stand justly condemned, deserving eternal death and separation from You. I loathe my sin, not merely because of all it has destroyed in my life, but because it is an offense to Your holiness! I long for Your tender mercy and undeserved forgiveness. I beg You to cleanse me and grant me pardon by the blood of Christ that I might serve Him as my Savior and Lord and ultimately be transformed into His likeness. And by Your power I commit myself to turning from my sin, forsaking it in every area of my life, and surrendering myself completely to Your Lordship. I want to be Your unworthy slave, and You to be my loving Master.

I would hasten to add that this should not be considered a "sinner's prayer" to be repeated in some perfunctory fashion, but rather a dramatized illustration of the dynamics occurring in the inner core of a person under deep conviction. This is what it means to enter the narrow gate. Moreover, we must be careful not to assume that every convert experiences the same level of remorse or contrition. Not everyone reacts with ebullition. For example, a child who has had far less opportunity to practice his sin and experience its devastations in life will not repent with the same level of intensity as a man seasoned in rebellion.

However, with these thoughts in mind, we find great comfort in yet another startling mystery of salvation, namely, *it is God who grants repentance* (Acts 5:31,11:18). He alone quickens the heart (John 1:13, 3:8; *cf.* Rom. 8:11; Titus 3:5) and gives the gift of faith (Phil. 1:29; 2 Peter 1:3), for it is always God's grace that is preeminent in salvation (*cf.* Rom. 3:20; Gal. 2:16). Although man is required by God to repent (Luke 13:3), ultimately it is God who graciously teaches him the terrible consequences of sin (Acts 17:31), and grants him "repentance leading to the knowledge of the truth" (2 Tim. 2:24, 25; *cf.* 2 Thess. 2:10).

Preaching Repentance in the Early Church

Examples of this kind of genuine, narrow-gate repentance can be seen all through Scripture. One powerful illustration is in Acts 2 when Peter preached to his Jewish compatriots and explained the supernatural events surrounding Pentecost. As the Jews stood dumfounded by the outpouring of the Holy Spirit, the apostle, speaking under the inspiration of the Holy Spirit, boldly blasted their pride and prejudice. Given the undeniable work of God they witnessed, the evidence was overwhelming: they were guilty of murdering their Messiah, Jesus of Nazareth, and were thereby objects of divine wrath. Peter condemned them as godless men who nailed Jesus to a cross (v. 23) and later said, "Therefore let all the house of Israel know for certain that God has made Him both Lord and Christ—this Jesus whom you crucified" (v. 36).

Upon hearing the divine verdict, the pain of genuine repentance struck them to the very core: "Now when they heard this, they were pierced to the heart, and said to Peter and the rest of the apostles, 'Brethren, what shall we do?'" (v. 37). In the original language, the phrase *pierced to the heart* describes a sudden severe pain as if stabbed in the heart. Everyone who has truly been born again knows this feeling. This is the Spirit-induced pain of unmitigated guilt and shame over sin, the sharp sting of conviction, the terrible ache of brokenness that will inevitably lead to bitter tears of repentance and a pleading for forgiveness.

Their pain caused them to cry out to Peter and the rest of the apostles, "Brethren, what shall we do?" (v. 37b). I fear that few who profess Christ have experienced anything close to this level of remorse over the heinousness of their sin and its inconceivable offense to a Holy God. Frankly, most professing Christians don't see what the big fuss is all about. They are convinced that they are just not that bad. This was certainly the attitude of the Jews who were by far the most fastidious religionists of their day. However, when a man fails to see his sin as God sees it—when his heart is never pierced with guilt—his perception of Christ's atoning work on the cross will be tragically deficient. Such ingratitude renders a man equally guilty of hanging the Savior on a tree. To be sure, such ungratefulness will inevitably lead to a religious house built upon the sand of self-effort that will someday be destroyed by a torrent of divine judgment.

Peter's response to their desperate query underscores the quintessential key to entering the narrow gate. He answered them and said, "Repent, and let each of you be baptized in the name of

Jesus Christ for the forgiveness of your sins" (v. 38). He called for them to be baptized in order to declare publicly their repentance, to acknowledge to all their Jewish friends and family that, despite their strict adherence to Judaism, they had repented of their sin and placed their faith in Jesus Christ who was the final sacrifice for sin and who alone could reconcile sinners to a holy God. By their baptism, they publicly identified with His death, burial, and resurrection—a public declaration that was certain to cost many of them their families, friends, careers, and, in some cases, their lives.

Repentance and the End of Self

Genuine salvation requires the *end* of self, not the *satisfaction* of self. We do not come to the Savior primarily to find fulfillment, happiness, or purpose in life (although those are secondary by-products). Nor do we come to achieve our greatest potential and satisfy our unmet needs and ambitions. Our greatest need is to be *forgiven, born again, justified, and thereby reconciled to a holy God* (John 3:1-21). We need to be saved from our inherent sinfulness that renders us guilty before a just and righteous God. We need to be reconciled to Him by faith in Christ who alone is our only hope of salvation. Therefore, we come to Christ begging for undeserved mercy, broken and contrite, pleading for forgiveness, mourning over our sin, deeply aware of the darkness of our depravity exposed by the light of God's holiness. Then, knowing that we are utterly incapable of contributing anything to our salvation, we plead the blood of Christ. Then, and only then, will He save us.

For this reason Jesus said, "Blessed are the poor in spirit, for theirs is the kingdom of heaven" (Matt. 5:3). The term "poor" comes from a Greek verb *ptochos* meaning "to grovel," "cower," or to "cringe like a beggar." It denotes one who shrinks or crouches back into a corner in absolute destitution like a penniless pauper; someone who has nothing, no means of support, utterly poverty stricken; one who cannot survive unless someone offers assistance. The point of Jesus' words could therefore be paraphrased this way:

> I will bless anyone who acknowledges that they have absolutely nothing they can offer to merit salvation. Those who admit that they are utterly dependent upon divine grace alone; who recognize they have no resources in themselves to find favor with Me

and who, therefore, stand before Me in utter desperation, humble of heart, empty handed, broken, bankrupt, convinced of their spiritual poverty.

Often the truly penitent will testify that in the midst of their anguish they became convinced that they were beyond the reach of divine grace. But thankfully, *never is a man closer to grace than when he is convinced he cannot attain it*. Only when he has no hope of saving himself can he be sure that God alone will save him. What a marvelous and inscrutable mystery this is: *the Holy Spirit brings us to the end of ourselves and makes the unwilling willing, and the dead alive.* To be sure, we have nothing to contribute to our salvation, thus we share in none of its glory. Indeed, "He saved us, not on the basis of deeds which we have done in righteousness, but according to His mercy, by the washing of regeneration and renewing by the Holy Spirit, whom He poured out upon us richly through Jesus Christ our Savior, so that being justified by His grace we might be made heirs according to the hope of eternal life" (Titus 3:5-7).

The Great Omission in Contemporary Evangelicalism

Perhaps the most obvious evidence of apostasy in contemporary evangelicalism can be seen more in what is *omitted* from the gospel message than what is *stated*. This is especially true as it relates to repentance. Seldom do we hear preachers calling people to repent of their sins and become a slave of Christ. If you go to a Christian bookstore and peruse the best sellers, you will be hard-pressed to find any mention of the word *repent*, and if you do, seldom will it be emphasized or explained biblically.

Yet when we examine the Scriptures, we see clearly that without repentance no person can be forgiven and enter the glory of heaven. It is not an exaggeration to say that repentance is the very key to the kingdom of heaven. When John the Baptist came to prepare the way of the Lord, he came "preaching a baptism of repentance for the forgiveness of sins" (Luke 3:3). As the last of the prophets, his message echoed the warnings of his ancient counterparts as Luke recorded quoting Isaiah 40:3-5: "The voice of one crying in the wilderness, 'make ready the way of the Lord, make His paths straight. Every ravine shall be filled up, and every mountain and hill shall be brought low; and the crooked shall become straight, and the rough roads smooth; and all flesh shall see the salvation of God'" (Luke 3:4-6). Here we understand that John the Baptist, like Isaiah before him, warned sinners to prepare the highway to their heart through repentance in order to receive the Messiah Savior and King.

Because the ancient people were accustomed to having a royal detachment go before a monarch and literally prepare the road for smooth passage, the inspired herald of Messiah used metaphoric language they could understand. John cried out to them the very essence of repentance:

> Your heart must be prepared to receive salvation. Fill up all the ravines that contain the filth of your lusts; fill up all the crevices of secret sin. Bring low the mountain peaks of self-righteousness and pride you have erected to exalt yourself. Humble yourself completely before the King. Straighten your crooked, twisted, and perverse attitudes and beliefs. Smooth out the rough roads of your sinful habits and fill up the potholes of temptation that cause you and others to stumble. Deal aggressively with every aspect of your life. Repent! And as a result of your repentance, "all flesh shall see the salvation of God" (Luke 3:6).

The centrality of repentance in the gospel can also be seen in the message Jesus preached. In fact, the opening word of His first sermon was "Repent, for the kingdom of heaven is at hand" (Matt. 4:17). Likewise, just before He ascended back into heaven, He miraculously opened the minds of His disciples so they would finally understand the fullness of His Person and work in light of the Old Testament, "that the Christ should suffer and rise again from the dead the third day; and that *repentance for forgiveness of sins should be proclaimed in His name to all the nations*" (Luke 24:46,47; emphasis mine). There can be no mistake: preaching repentance for the remission of sin was fundamental to the message of Christ. He opened with it, and He closed with it.

Salvation comes only to those who recognize their desperate need for forgiveness and, on that basis, willingly turn from their sin. Jesus underscored this truth when He said to the self-righteous Pharisees, "It is not those who are well who need a physician, but those who are sick. I have not come to call the righteous but sinners to repentance" (Luke 5:32). Here He speaks strong words concerning those who perceive themselves to be righteous and are therefore blind to their need for repentance. Instead, His message of good news is for those who confess their sin and plead for undeserved forgiveness. Later Jesus went on to say, "I tell you that in the same way, there will be more joy in heaven over one sinner who repents, than over ninety-nine righteous persons who need no repentance . . . . I tell you, there is joy in the presence of the angels of God over one sinner who repents" (Luke 15:7,10).

6

Marks of Genuine Repentance

Over the years, I have become increasingly convinced that many more Christians would be willing to preach repentance if they better understood its nature and power. Thankfully, God has not left us without insight on this issue. Perhaps the most succinct summary of the doctrine of repentance is found in Paul's words to the Corinthians in 2 Corinthians 7. There, he describes their godly reaction to a severe letter of rebuke he had written to them earlier confronting them for tolerating false teachers who had taken up residence within the church and had viciously slandered him. Undoubtedly, this was the "thorn in the flesh, a messenger of Satan" that Paul implored the Lord three times to remove (2 Cor. 12:7-10). Upon hearing Titus' encouraging report concerning their contrition, Paul's joyful description of their reaction gives us profound insight into what real repentance looks like when a *believer* is confronted with sin.

We can hear the relief in Paul's words when he wrote,

> But God, who comforts the depressed, comforted us by the coming of Titus; and not only by his coming, but also by the comfort with which he was comforted in you, as he reported to us your longing, your mourning, your zeal for me; so that I rejoiced even more. For though I caused you sorrow by my letter, I do not regret it; though I did regret it—for I see that that letter caused you sorrow, though only for a while—I now rejoice, not that you were made sorrowful, but that you were made sorrowful to the point of repentance; for you were made sorrowful according to the will of God, so that you might not suffer loss in anything through us (2 Cor. 7:6-9).

True Christian love will never avoid confronting sin for fear of reprisal. Paul took that risk. Although he regretted the sorrow that he knew it would bring to those he loved, his concern for their spiritual blessing transcended his fear of further rejection. Because of God's convicting grace, their hearts were tender to the truth—they received his stinging rebuke that brought temporary sorrow, a convicting remorse that "made them sorrowful to the point of repentance" (v. 9). Because they "were made sorrowful according to the will of God" (v. 9), they responded to His work of grace in their hearts, acknowledged their guilt, and decisively committed themselves to turn from their sin, come what may.

Although their repentance had temporal implications in that it restored God's blessing upon them personally and corporately as a church—not to mention their restoration with Paul—it also prevented the forfeiture of eternal reward as indicated by the statement, "so that you might not suffer loss in anything through us" (v. 9). Every Christian should share this kind of concern for the brethren.

Paul went on to describe the shame and remorse that will inevitably accompany genuine repentance: "For the sorrow that is according to the will of God produces a repentance without regret, leading to salvation, but the sorrow of the world produces death" (v. 10). To be sure, as we have discussed earlier, a person must first repent of his or her sins to be saved—indeed, this results in a gift of grace that is "without regret." Such humble contrition will then manifest itself in subsequent encounters with indwelling sin. When a believer repents, he experiences something far different than "the sorrow of the world [that] produces death" (v. 10). His godly sorrow causes him to mourn over offending God more than getting caught. He feels the pain of dishonoring God more than personal embarrassment. He hates his sin more than the stress it produced. Moreover, he longs for forgiveness, reconciliation, and spiritual blessing more than life itself. John MacArthur explained it well when he said,

> True biblical repentance is not psychological, emotional human remorse, seeking merely to relieve stress and improve one's circumstances. Though it inevitably produces the fruit of a changed life (*cf.* Matt. 3:8; Luke 3:8; Acts 26:20), it is not behavioral, but spiritual. The *sorrow of the world*—remorse, wounded pride, self-pity, unfulfilled hopes—has no healing power, no transforming, saving, or redeeming capability. It *produces* guilt, shame, resentment, anguish, despair, depression, hopelessness, even, as in the case of Judas (Matt. 27:3-5), *death*.[8]

We find great encouragement in Paul's description of the marks of genuine repentance that he witnessed in the lives of his beloved Corinthians. He summarized them when he said, "For behold what earnestness this very thing, this godly sorrow, had produced in you: what vindication of yourselves, what indignation, what fear, what longing, what zeal, what avenging of wrong" (2 Cor. 7:11). Herein is the fruit of repentance.

As we examine verse 11, we see first the "earnestness" of their "godly sorrow": their solemn sincerity about turning from sin. It was eager, aggressive, and serious above all else. They did not deal with their sin with a cavalier attitude, but rather they manifested the same kind of conviction as found in the plaintive confession of David in Psalm 51, where he pleaded:

> Be gracious to me, O God, according to Your lovingkindness; according to the greatness of Your compassion blot out my transgressions. Wash me thoroughly from my iniquity, and cleanse me from my sin. For I know my transgressions, and my sin is ever before me. Against You, You only, I have sinned, and done what is evil in Your sight, so that You are justified when You speak, and blameless when You judge (vv. 1-4).

This is also seen in Peter's earnest repentance when, after denying the Lord three times, the cock crowed and "he went out and wept bitterly" (Matt. 26:75). Yet, as with the Corinthians, and as with David, because of his godly sorrow, the Lord forgave him and restored him to fellowship and lavished upon him unimaginable spiritual blessings—a magnificent picture of the Lord's merciful and compassionate response to repentance.

Paul went on in v. 11 to rejoice over their repentance saying, "what vindication of yourselves," denoting their desire to do all they could to make things right, to clear their name, and to make a new name for themselves that glorified God. He continued his praise saying, "what indignation," indicating their utter contempt for sin, their loathing of it, and their resentment for rebelling against God. They felt a sense of anger over offending a holy God, the Lover of their souls, as well as bringing reproach upon the Lord, themselves, their families, and their church. This is what we must look for in genuine repentance.

But Paul did not stop there; his observations animated him to further praise when he said, "what fear" (v. 11), referring to their appropriate fear of God, their profound, reverential awe for the One they worshipped. He went on to remark in v. 11, "what longing," indicating their passion to once again enjoy sweet fellowship with God and with him; "what zeal," signifying their willingness to surrender themselves to the will of God and please Him at all cost; "what avenging of wrong," referring to their commitment to make things right, to be reconciled with those *against whom* they had sinned, as well as with those *with whom* they had sinned. This is the stuff of genuine repentance: *it is a hatred of sin, a turning from sin, and a determination to forsake sin that is so strong as to dominate every thought and to direct every act.*

Every Christian should take great comfort in understanding that his repentance is never perfect. Repentance grows over time as we become more conformed to the image of Christ. From the very first moment of conversion until his final breath, a Christian is always examining his heart in repentance (1 John 1:9). As he grows in the grace and knowledge of Christ, he understands more fully the depth and breadth of his sin. While his hatred of sin grows, he becomes increasingly vigilant in finding more pockets of rebellion in his heart and seeks more opportunities to turn from that which he abhors. And when the final days of life draw near, he does not rest on the laurels of past victories and neither does he slow his pace, but rather he strains at the finish line in an effort to forsake remaining sin all the more.

May we examine our hearts in the light of Scripture to see if indeed our repentance is real, and our faith is genuine. And for those whom "the Spirit Himself testifies with our spirit that we are children of God" (Rom. 8:16), may we rejoice knowing that the Author of life has granted us "the repentance that leads to life" (Acts 11:18).

7

Eternal Wrath and Grace

From the outset, we must understand that the wrath of God and His purposes in eternal punishment are infinitely beyond our ability to understand. We who are least holy cannot comprehend God who is most holy. For this reason, we must bow in utmost humility before His omniscience, for He has said, "'My thoughts are not your thoughts, nor are your ways My way,' says the Lord" (Isa. 55:8). This awe-inspiring reality must therefore rule our heart as we attempt to examine His Word on the matter.

But it is also important to acknowledge that God is not ambiguous regarding the inevitability of eternal punishment for sin. Because God is holy, all sin must be punished; therefore, the wicked must receive retribution for their deeds (Luke 12:47-48).

Sinners can either trust in Christ as the Substitute who paid the penalty for their sins on the cross, or they can reject His offer of grace and pay for their own sins throughout eternity. As cited earlier, unbelievers "shall be cast out into the outer darkness; in that place there shall be weeping and gnashing of teeth" (Matt. 8:12). Jesus promised that He will one day say to the wicked, "Depart from Me, accursed ones, into the eternal fire which has been prepared for the devil and his angels . . . these will go away into eternal punishment, but the righteous into eternal life" (Matt. 25:41, 46).

God has promised to "[deal] out retribution to those who do not know God and to those who do not obey the gospel of our Lord Jesus. These will pay the penalty of eternal destruction, away from the presence of the Lord and from the glory of His power" (2 Thess. 1:8,9). The term "destruction" (*olethros*, used also in 1 Thess. 5:3) does not refer to *annihilation*, but to *ruination*—the loss of all things that give worth to our existence (*cf.* 1 Tim. 6:9). The same term is used in 1 Corinthians 5:5 in the context of delivering an immoral man over to Satan (excommunicating him from the church) "for the destruction of his flesh, so that his spirit may be saved in the day of the Lord Jesus." Obviously the man's flesh did not cease to exist. What He is saying is that by being thrust out of the fellowship of the church and into the realm of Satan, he would *suffer* under the weight of divine chastening, the tool God would use to bring conviction and repentance to his heart.

Other passages referring to the "destruction" of the wicked use a similar term (*apoleia; cf.* Phil. 3:19; 2 Peter 3:7) that can also be translated "ruin" or "waste." The same term was used in Mark 14:4 to speak of what some considered the "waste" of the expensive perfume poured over Jesus' head. Once again, the precious ointment did not cease to exist, but rather it was "destroyed" or "ruined" in the sense that it would never again be able to be used as it was originally intended.

So the idea of "the penalty of eternal destruction" (2 Thess. 1:9) speaks of an eternal state of conscious suffering where the lost will experience the utter hopelessness, barrenness, and worthlessness of their existence. Their total existence will be destroyed, ruined, wasted—a reality that will fuel their eternal blasphemy, thus the words of our Lord, "Let the one who does wrong, still do wrong; and the one who is filthy, still be filthy" (Rev. 22:11). The inconceivable bleakness of their eternal state will characterize their destruction and be the source of their fury. For this reason, they will live forever "away from the presence of the Lord and from the glory of His power" (2 Thess. 1:9).

This place of torment is described by Isaiah as a place of "devouring fire" and "everlasting burning" (33:14)—a place where Jesus said the wicked will be "[thrown] . . . into the furnace of fire. In that place there will be weeping and gnashing of teeth" (Matt. 13:42; *cf.* v. 50). This is clearly a state of unending conscious torment where unbelievers "will be tormented day and night forever and ever" (Rev. 20:10), where "the smoke of their torment goes up forever and ever; and they have no rest, day or night" (14:11).

Jesus refers to hell as a place of "unquenchable fire" (Mark 9:43), "where their worm does not die" (v. 48). This strongly refutes the notion of annihilation where some people would argue that the wicked will experience the wrath of God only temporarily and then simply cease to exist. Such a doctrine is impossible to harmonize with Jesus' parable of the rich man and Lazarus that also underscores the conscious and eternal punishment of unbelievers:

> Now the poor man died and was carried away by the angels to Abraham's bosom; and the rich man also died and was buried. In Hades he lifted up his eyes, being in torment, and saw Abraham far away and Lazarus in his bosom. And he cried out and said, "Father

Abraham, have mercy on me, and send Lazarus so that he may dip the tip of his finger in water and cool off my tongue, for I am in agony in this flame" (Luke 16:22-24).

Such a horrifying fate not only underscores God's utter hatred of sin, but also his great love for sinners. The apostle Paul summarizes this in a most moving way:

> But God demonstrates His own love toward us, in that while we were yet sinners, Christ died for us. Much more then, having now been justified by His blood, we shall be saved from the wrath of God through Him. For if while we were enemies we were reconciled to God through the death of His Son, much more, having been reconciled, we shall be saved by His life. And not only this, but we also exult in God through our Lord Jesus Christ, through whom we have now received the reconciliation (Rom. 5:8-11).

May our awareness of what we deserve humble us in what we have received in Christ, and with the hymnist sing:

Praise to the Lord, the Almighty, the King of creation!
O my soul, praise Him, for He is thy health and salvation!
All ye who hear, now to His temple draw near;
Praise Him in glad adoration.

Praise to the Lord, Who over all things so wondrously reigneth;
Shelters thee under His wings, yea, so gently sustaineth!
Hast thou not seen how thy desires ever have been
Granted in what He ordaineth?

Praise to the Lord, Who hath fearfully, wondrously, made thee;
Health hath vouchsafed and, when heedlessly falling, hath stayed thee.
What need or grief ever hath failed of relief?
Wings of His mercy did shade thee.

Praise to the Lord, Who doth prosper thy work and defend thee;
Surely His goodness and mercy here daily attend thee.
Ponder anew what the Almighty can do,
If with His love He befriend thee.

*Praise to the Lord, Who, when tempests their
warfare are waging,
Who, when the elements madly around thee are
raging,
Biddeth them cease, turneth their fury to peace,
Whirlwinds and waters assuaging.*

*Praise to the Lord, Who, when darkness of sin
is abounding,
Who, when the godless do triumph, all virtue
confounding,
Sheddeth His light, chaseth the horrors of night,
Saints with His mercy surrounding.*

*Praise to the Lord, O let all that is in me adore
Him!
All that hath life and breath, come now with
praises before Him.
Let the Amen sound from His people again,
Gladly for aye we adore Him.*
—Joachim Neander

Endnotes

1   Elon Foster, *New Cyclopedia of Prose Illustrations* (New York: T.Y. Crowell, 1877), 696.

2   Wm. G. T. Shedd, *Theological Essays*, (Solid Ground Christian Books; reprint, Scribner, Armstrong and Co., 1877), 264.

3   A.W.Tozer, *The Knowledge of the Holy*, (HarperCollins Publishers, New York, 1961), vii.

4   Technically there were a total of twelve Sabbaths, including the seventh day Sabbath. Eight were a sequence of holy convocations and feasts: Passover (Exod. 12:1-14); Unleavened Bread (Ex. 12:15- 20); Firstfruits (Lev. 23:9-14); Pentecost (Harvest or Weeks) (Deut. 16:9-12); Trumpets, Rosh Hashanah (Num. 29:1-6); Day of Atonement, Yom Kippur (Lev. 23:26-32); Booths (Tabernacles or Ingathering) (Neh. 8:13-18). The New Moon Sabbath (Num. 28:11) could be considered a tenth Sabbath, and finally, Leviticus 25 gives a prescription for two more Sabbaths, the Sabbatic Year and Year of Jubilee, making a total of twelve Sabbaths.

5   Alva J. McClain, *The Greatness of the Kingdom: An Inductive Study of the Kingdom of God*, (BMH Books, Winona Lake, Indiana, 1959), 65.

6   John Owen, *The Nature, Power, Deceit, and Prevalency of Indwelling Sin (1667)*; reprinted in: *Overcoming Sin and*

Temptation: Three Classic Works by John Owen, (Crossway Books, Wheaton, Illinois, 2006), 247.

7   D. Martyn Lloyd-Jones, *Studies in the Sermon on the Mount* (Grand Rapids: Eerdmans, 1959), 2:248.

8   John MacArthur, *The MacArthur New Testament Commentary: 2 Corinthians* (Moody Publishers, Chicago, Illinois, 2003) 266.

CPSIA information can be obtained
at www.ICGtesting.com
Printed in the USA
LVHW081209110420
653044LV00006B/57

9 781734 345209